rounds

Rounds is a series of circular characters whose real-life stories start where they end which is why they are called

rounds

which is why they are called Rounds is a series of circular characters whose real-life stories start where they end

To Lewis, with love

First published 2016 by Nosy Crow Ltd
The Crow's Nest, 10a Lant Street
London SE1 1QR
www.nosycrow.com

ISBN 978 0 85763 559 4 (HB)
ISBN 978 0 85763 560 0 (PB)

Nosy Crow and associated logos are trademarks
and/or registered trademarks of Nosy Crow Ltd.

Concept and story research by Barry Tranter and Emma Tranter
Text © Emma Tranter 2016
Illustrations © Barry Tranter 2016
Consultant: Chris Jarvis, Education Officer at the
Oxford University Museum of Natural History

The right of Emma Tranter to be identified as the author and Barry Tranter
to be identified as the illustrator of this work has been asserted.

A CIP catalogue record for this book is available from the British Library.

Printed in China by Imago

Papers used by Nosy Crow are made
from wood grown in sustainable forests.

1 3 5 7 9 8 6 4 2 (HB)
1 3 5 7 9 8 6 4 2 (PB)

Cora
Caterpillar

Let's eat!

Barry Tranter

nosy crow

Emma Tranter

A caterpillar is a baby moth or butterfly.

Meet Cora. Cora is a caterpillar.
Here she is sitting on a leaf.
Cora loves munching on juicy green leaves.

Caterpillars have long, soft bodies.

Hello, I'm Cora. Nice to meet you!

There are lots of different types of caterpillar. Cora is a Monarch.

Caterpillars live all over the world.

Cora crawls along very slowly. But she is a great climber – she can even walk upside down!

Up I go!

Caterpillars crawl by moving their front half forwards before their back half follows.

Towards the back of their bodies, caterpillars have eight sucker-like legs to help them climb.

Caterpillars have six bendy legs at the front of their bodies.

She eats and eats . . .

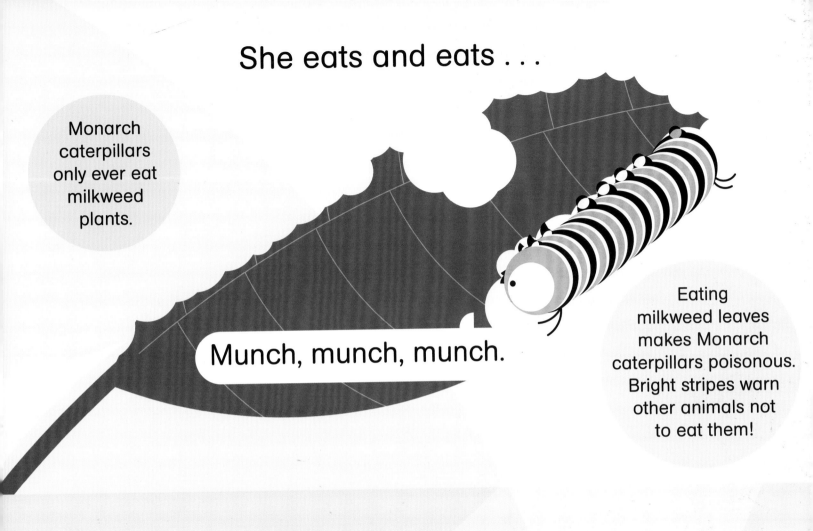

Monarch caterpillars only ever eat milkweed plants.

Munch, munch, munch.

Eating milkweed leaves makes Monarch caterpillars poisonous. Bright stripes warn other animals not to eat them!

. . . and eats some more!

I'm nice and full now!

The more caterpillars eat, the bigger they grow.

As Cora eats more, she keeps outgrowing her skin! Every time this happens, her old skin splits open and Cora crawls out in a new, bigger skin.

I'm starting to wriggle out.

My skin is very tight.

When an animal sheds its skin, it is called moulting.

When Cora is two weeks old, she finds a nice, safe place. It's time for her to turn into a butterfly!

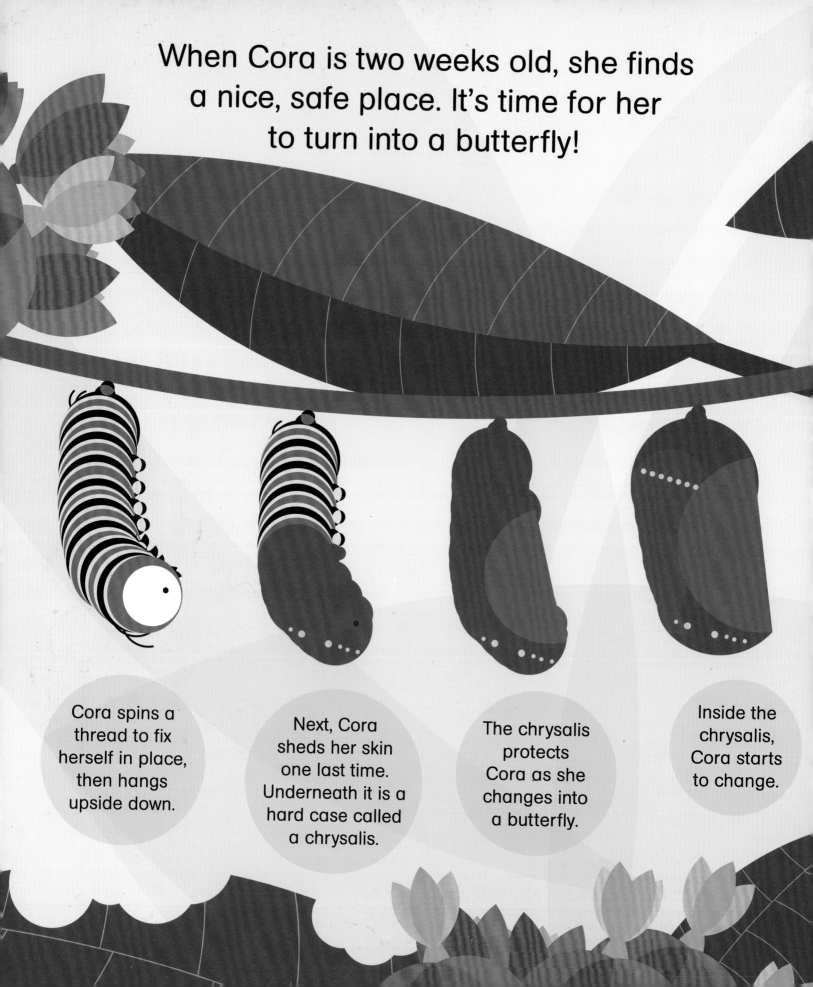

Cora spins a thread to fix herself in place, then hangs upside down.

Next, Cora sheds her skin one last time. Underneath it is a hard case called a chrysalis.

The chrysalis protects Cora as she changes into a butterfly.

Inside the chrysalis, Cora starts to change.

Cora is now a grown-up butterfly with beautiful patterned wings.

It takes three to four hours for new butterflies to dry their wings before they can fly.

I just can't wait to fly!

Butterflies are insects. All adult insects have six legs, wings and feelers on their heads.

She lets her wings dry before
flying for the first time.

Monarch
butterflies flap
their wings up
to 12 times
per second.

Most
butterflies fly
during the
day and rest
at night.

As a butterfly, Cora spends her time flitting from flower to flower to eat.

All butterflies have a long, strawlike mouth called a proboscis, which they use to suck up food.

When a butterfly is not feeding, its proboscis stays curled up.

She's on the hunt for nectar – the delicious, sugary liquid made inside flowers.

Butterflies can only eat liquid food.

Mmm . . . yummy nectar!

Butterflies can smell nectar through their feet and through the feelers on their heads.

Even though Monarch butterflies are poisonous to most animals, some birds and mice can still eat them. Watch out, Cora!

Animals that eat Monarch butterflies don't usually die, but they do feel sick.

Eeeek!

Some flies and wasps attack butterflies, too.

Cora must also take care when it's raining, as her wings are easily damaged.

Strong winds are also dangerous for butterflies.

I don't like this weather.

Butterflies usually shelter under a leaf when it is raining.

As soon as she can fly properly, Cora starts to look for a mate.

Male Monarchs have a black spot on each wing.

The black spot gives off a special smell to attract female butterflies.

Which of these males will I choose?

Here comes Carlton.
He is a male Monarch butterfly.

Hello, there. I'm Carlton.
You seem nice!

Female butterflies chase male butterflies through the air.

Hello, I like the way you smell!

After mating, Cora lays lots of tiny eggs.
She sticks them to the underside of
leaves where they will be safely out of sight.

Some Monarch butterflies lay about 1,000 eggs in their lifetime!

Butterflies lay their eggs on the type of leaf that caterpillars eat when they are born.

As the caterpillar grows inside the egg, the case becomes see-through.

I want my breakfast!

After two weeks, the caterpillar will be ready to change into a butterfly.

Newly-hatched Monarchs have pale grey stripes.

Four days later, Cora's eggs start to hatch.
Out pops a tiny baby caterpillar.
And she's very hungry!

As soon as they hatch, caterpillars eat their own egg cases.

Meet Caitlin, Cora's daughter. Caitlin is a caterpillar. Here she is sitting on a leaf. Caitlin loves munching on juicy green leaves.

Most Monarchs live for around six weeks.

Hello, I'm Caitlin. Nice to meet you!

There are about 20,000 species of butterflies and moths around the world.

Humans have about 650 muscles, while caterpillars have about 4,000.

The life cycle of a caterpillar

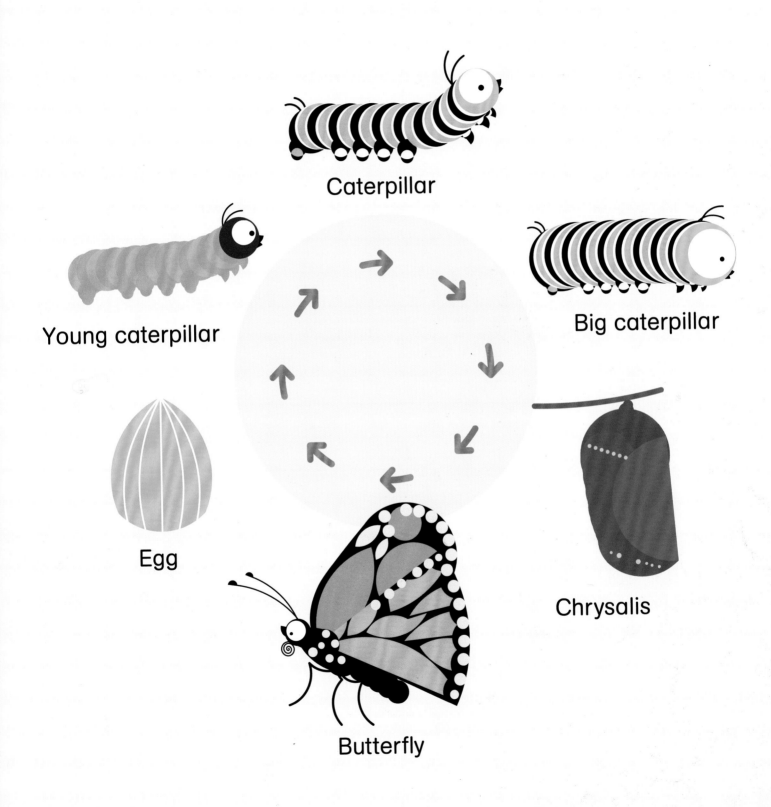

Caterpillar

Young caterpillar

Big caterpillar

Egg

Chrysalis

Butterfly

rounds

Rounds is a series of circular characters whose real-life stories start where they end which is why they are called

Rounds is a series of circular characters whose real-life stories start where they end which is why they are called